Blueprints

A Guide For 16 Independent Study Projects

Prufrock Press Inc.
P.O. Box 8813
Waco, TX 76714-8813
Phone: (800) 998-2208
Fax: (800) 240-0333
http://www.prufrock.com

Contents

Introduction

How many times has it happened in your classroom? You give your class an assignment that involves doing a long-term project. You let them choose the topic or subject that they would like to study. You give them a due date and even provide in-class time to work on the project. On the date that the project is to be completed, you find that a few students got half way through the project and gave up, a few more waited until the night before the project was due and put in one last-ditch effort to put together something that would meet the minimum requirements, and a few others have a glittering project that shows no evidence of learning. What went wrong? How could able students who seemed so excited about studying their chosen topics not have enough enthusiasm to carry them to the end of the project.

Projects and People

There are many different kinds of people in this world with varying temperaments and modes of learning and working. Some are goal-oriented, others are more concerned with the process than the end product; some are perfectionists, and others are lackadaisical; some are thinkers, and others are doers. While many students may be excited at the beginning of a learning project, for one reason or another, they may fail to complete the project or fall short of the expected learning that should have resulted from such a project.

Too often students are assigned or select to do a study project that is open-ended and vague. The assignments are often worded something like this:

"Make a model that shows all the parts."
"Write a paper that reflects your thoughts ."
"Make a game that would teach your classmates about this topic."
"Organize a debate that shows both sides of the issue."
"Write a story that includes as much factual information as possible. Present it as a skit."

These assignments are good, because they leave room for individual exploration and interpretation. The only problem is that often students get bogged down in the organizational aspects of the project and never achieve a satisfactory conclusion. This is as discouraging for the student as it is frustrating for the teacher.

Getting From Here to There

Obviously, or maybe not so obviously, completing a project is not just a matter of enthusiasm, interest, self-selection, motivation, or good intentions. Reaching your goal (or the teacher's goal) is also a matter of good planning and organization. It involves a complicated set of behaviors and processes that defines where you are, where you are going, and what all the steps are between here and there. Most often, we give students the end goal and expect them to fill in all the intermediary steps. We may, in fact, be expecting too much of children if we ask them to have the organizational skills to plan and carry out a project from beginning to end. While these are skills we would like them to acquire, the lack of these skills should not interfere with their learning experiences in the meantime.

Blueprints takes the guesswork out of independent or assigned study projects. It is a step-by-step guide to projects—how to select study topics, how to gather information, and how to communicate ideas and information to other people. It says to the student, "Here you are, there is your goal, and here's how you get to that goal." It takes a basic planning process and applies it to school projects, thus giving students a framework for learning and creating.

For the Instructor

Organizing for Action

The key component in this book is **organization**—laying out what needs to be done and tackling tasks in a systematic manner. By giving students an organizational framework to work within they can easily accomplish their goal while practicing these important skills. Through the process of collecting, organizing and sharing information, students should accomplish these goals:

- learn how to find and collect information
- learn how to organize information
- learn how to communicate information in various ways
- learn how to organize time and resources
- learn how to evaluate learning
- learn how to structure learning experiences
- learn how to think creatively
- find ways to meet personal needs to know about the world
- improve organizational skills that lead to accomplishment of long-term goals.

Blueprint Benefits

Blueprints presents a sequence of steps for each learning project that takes the learner from defining a study topic to presenting the final project and evaluating his/her project. This process of structuring individual learning projects has several advantages or benefits for both the instructor and the learner. They are:

- Projects are open-ended to allow for individual interpretation, needs, and interests.
- Guidelines assure that students have accomplished the educational goals of acquiring knowledge and processing information.
- Students learn and practice the skills of planning and organization—skills that they can then apply to other life and learning situations.
- Finished products will be a better quality than if planning had not been a part of the process.
- By providing students the necessary organization for planning a project, they can use their energy for increased learning, problem solving, creative thinking, and a polished presentation.
- Skeptical parents and administrators can be assured that some structure and direction is being given for projects, providing for specific learning objectives, acquisition of knowledge, and development of skills.
- The process gives a uniform standard for all students in terms of the scope of the project and the expected procedures and outcomes.
- Teachers have built-in checks of students' progress.

- The guidelines provide a set of interim goals for students to work toward, providing many opportunities for evaluation, changes, checks, and positive reinforcement along the way.
- The process prevents (or at least reduces) last minute changes in projects. Because everything has been carefully thought out beforehand, students know early in the project if it will work or not.

Classroom Applications

Blueprints has many applications in the classroom. These include the following:

1. Teachers can use the guidelines to structure research projects in subject areas by defining the specific areas that students are to research. The instructor might ask all students to produce a book of poems following a poetry unit, or a written report on something about South America, or a solution to a local problem.
2. The projects can, additionally, be used by individuals or small groups of students working independently on study projects that supplement or replace regular assignments. In this way, the instructor can guide students' independent study with a minimum of supervision.
3. The projects can also be used with an entire class to facilitate a variety of projects on topics in the same subject areas. An example of this would be if the class were studying the Renaissance Period, some students could produce a special event, some a debate, some a learning center, and others a book.
4. Another variation would be to use the project guidelines to structure a situation where all students are doing the same project (a game, for instance) in the same subject area (like science) but with different study topics (crystals, whales, mammals, simple machines, etc.).

Each project outline is specific enough to get students from the beginning to the end, but general enough so that instructors can use the outlines in a variety of situations. Additional information is provided for each project that suggests several possibilities for using the project in classrooms. In addition to these, instructors will undoubtedly find many unique ways to implement the project plans.

Adding Restrictions

Blueprints offers teachers flexibility in determining how each project is completed. Some teachers may feel comfortable with letting some students proceed entirely on their own with very little direction. Other teachers may want to add guidelines or restrictions to the basic outline for more control over the types of projects that

students complete and the kinds of learning that take place along the way. Teachers may add requirements and structure to the projects in the following ways:
- specifying how much research must be completed
- adding due dates or time limits for some of the tasks
- putting an * by some of the tasks and indicating that work must be checked with the teacher at this point and the teacher must sign the assignment sheet before proceeding
- putting limitations or guidelines on the scope of the project (subject areas, study topics, etc.)
- specifying the criteria for evaluation
- requiring a written bibliography
- requiring that research notes or other procedural tasks are handed in with the final project
- limit choices for the final product
- requiring use of a variety of resources
- encouraging questions or study topics that necessitate original thinking on the part of the student.

In addition to determining the scope and timing of the project, the role of the instructor in the projects is to:
- check on progress
- help solve problems
- help select and arrange for resources
- encourage
- help students add their own original ideas
- evaluate.

The Basic Plan

All projects in this book involve a similar process or format. One of the major objectives of this process is to add to, supplement, or enrich students' existing knowledge while building research and organizational skills. For this reason the process combines research with opportunities for individual interpretations or explorations. The basic process is as follows:
1. Topic Selection
2. Assessing present knowledge
3. Narrowing the topic using questions or subtopics
4. Selecting sources of information
5. Collecting information
6. Organizing information
7. Preparing information for presentation
   - planning project
   - getting help (if needed)
   - getting materials
   - making project
   - making necessary changes or revisions
8. Making presentation
9. Evaluation
10. Application - extending knowledge, stretching thinking.

Evaluation

An important part of each learning experience is evaluation. This is the final step in bringing closure to the project. Typically the teacher does the evaluating, but it is just as valuable and appropriate to involve the student in the evaluation process.

Because each instructor has different goals for each learning experience, evaluation of the projects will involve different criteria. For this reason, evaluation forms have not been provided for each project. Instead, a blank evaluation form has been included. Additionally, suggestions for each project include ideas for evaluation. These are only suggestions, so teachers may use any criteria that they find appropriate and add any additional criteria that are related to their goals for the project.

Suggestions for Projects

The teacher will undoubtedly find many applications for the project outlines. This section, however, gives suggestions for various uses for each project. Also included in this section are possible criteria for evaluating each project.

Book

For anyone who has any doubts, it should be stated that writing a book is as educational as writing a report but is much more motivating. Students find it gratifying to see that their efforts have resulted in a bound book. It is something that they will save for years. The contents of the book can be factual or fiction. In either case, students will be doing research, assessing their audience, practicing composition skills, and thinking creatively. You may use this assignment to have all students in your class produce books on various topics or as an extension for an existing unit of study. Whether students write story books for younger students, how-to-do-it books, factual books, or historical novels, you can be sure that they will take pride in the finished product.

Criteria for evaluation:
- Did the student make wise use of time?
- Is the topic and reading level appropriate for the intended audience?
- Is the text well-written?
- Did the student use imagination?
- Is the book graphically attractive?
- Is the research evident?
- Is the book factual?
- Is the book something that children will enjoy reading?
- Is there a well-developed plot?
- Does the author use descriptive words?
- Is the cover attractive?
- Is the book well-organized?

Debate

A debate is the ultimate challenge in terms of extensive research, impeccable organization, and a polished presentation. For this reason, this project is probably best used with older students. Topics for debates may fall into a variety of categories, but should fulfill the following qualifications:
1. They should be of a significant nature, affecting a large number of people.
2. They must be within the boundaries of governmental jurisdiction.
3. They should be current and generate widespread media coverage.

4. They must be durable. They should not quickly pass from public interest.
5. They must be debatable. That is, they should have valid issues on both sides.

Rather than suggesting propositions which may be outdated by the time this project is used, it would be better if instructors use these guidelines in conjunction with up-to-date media sources to select timely, significant debate topics for their classes. In selecting topics, instructors should keep in mind that there are three kinds of propositions:
1. Fact - This is usually an objective, verifiable statement. It is the least controversial of the three propositions.
2. Value - This is a statement that reflects our judgements about the qualities of something.
3. Policy - This statement outlines considerations of a course of action or law that will guide present and future decisions.

Criteria for evaluation:
- Has the problem been accurately analyzed?
- Did the team conduct thorough research?
- Did the team explore all possible arguments?
- Are the arguments backed up with authoritative facts?
- Is research up-to-date?
- Are the arguments valid?
- Does the proof of position include a combination of reasoning and evidence?
- Is the presentation polished?
- Is the presentation persuasive?
- Is the presentation organized?
- Are team members able to refute opposition's arguments?
- Is the debate conducted in a professional manner?

Demonstration

The demonstration project offers students the opportunity to practice organizational and speech skills while sharing something that they know how to do. You will find that the students in your room are "experts" in a variety of fields. Being able to share this expertise is validating for the student who is making the presentation and educational for the rest of the class. Students will not only learn about each other, they will be introduced to a

large variety of information. Because the student selects something that he/she already knows how to do, there is not as much research required for this project as for other projects. Each presentation will be more interesting, however, if students can add information and facts to the essential steps the one follows. For this reason, students will need to conduct some research. Students might want to consider some of these ideas for demonstrations:
- how to program a computer
- how to tell time using the sun
- how to collect solar energy
- how to build a bird house and attract birds
- how to plant a terrarium
- how to solve an algebraic equation
- how to bisect an angle
- how to macrame
- how to put on skiis
- how to change a tire on a bike
- how to identify rocks
- how to make an electrical circuit
- how to make chocolate chip cookies
- how to do the five basic ballet positions
- how to use an abacus
- how to arrange flowers.

Criteria for evaluation:
- Did the student pick a topic that was appropriate for a demonstration?
- Did the student complete adequate research?
- Did the student demonstrate stated objectives?
- Was the presentation clear, well-organized, and easy to follow?
- Was the information complete?
- Was the presentation interesting to the audience?
- Was the presentation educational?
- Did the student use good speech techniques?
- Were the materials organized and ready for use?

Display Project

This is a very versatile project because it includes several different types of displays and it is adaptable to a variety of subjects. Students may present the information from their study units in the form of a bulletin board, an idea cube, or a display of artifacts, specimens, or collections. Almost any unit of study could culminate in a display of information, such as:

- How simple machines work
- Poems of a favorite author
- An illustration of a historic event or place
- Costumes of a certain period
- Systems of the body
- Endangered animals
- Examples of geometric solids
- Categories of plants, animals, tools, types of houses, or symbols
- History of a holiday, an area, or social phenomenon

- A historical timeline of the development of continents, evolution of animals, movement of people, or increase in population
- Biographical sketches of famous people
- Illustration of cycles like money circulation, geological movements, plant growth, life cycles, animal migrations, or recycling paper
- Examples of propaganda, advertising, or art from a specific era
- Instructions for caring for plants, introducing a bill to congress, conducting a scientific experiment, folding origami, or dissecting a fish.

Criteria for evaluation:
- Did the student make good use of time?
- Does the project show adequate research?
- Does the display present useful, interesting information?
- Is the display a learning device for other people?
- Is the display attractive and carefully constructed?
- Is the display attention-getting?
- Does the project show creativity?
- Does the display contain a variety of presentation techniques?
- Is the display visible from a distance?
- Does the display create interest in the topic?

Experiment

Experiments typically are used to test some scientific principle or phenomenon. Students should not have any problems finding scientific questions that they can test. Questions need not, however, be difficult. Students can gain the same skills in experimentation by testing the acidity of various substances as they can by breaking water into components of oxygen and hydrogen. The key to selecting a question for experimentation is that it is something that the student is interested in, that it requires testing, and that it is challenging.

Some sample questions might be:
- Which brand of hamburger contains the most meat?
- What conditions are important for predicting weather in our area?
- What additive best preserves cut flowers?
- What is the effect of colored lights on plant growth?
- How does the angle of inclination affect the distance a model car will travel?
- Which metal rusts most quickly?
- How does the angle of projection affect the flight of an airplane?
- Does talking to plants affect their growth?
- Which sunscreen is most effective in blocking out the sun's rays?
- How do different reinforcers affect learning rates in rats?

This project may also be used to test principles or phenomena in the social sciences. In this case, students would most likely be using people as their subjects. The problem with experiments in the social sciences is that it is difficult to get rid of all the factors that affect behavior but which are not part of the hypothesis. For this reason, experiments in the social sciences tend to be rather sophisticated and are probably better left to older students. Some possible questions for experimentation would be:

- How does room lighting affect mood?
- What is the usual distance between people when they converse?
- How does watching television affect school learning?
- How does advertising affect product recognition?
- Which color is most effective in advertising?
- How does the rate of inflation affect spending for non-necessity items?
- How does year-round school affect learning?
- How does self-concept affect learning?

Criteria for evaluation:
- Did the student make good use of time?
- Was the question selected for experimentation appropriate?
- Did the experiment answer the question?
- Was only one variable tested?
- Was the experiment carefully executed?
- Were the results accurately recorded?
- Was the conclusion valid?
- Was the data organized in a graph or chart?
- Was evidence supplied to justify conclusion?
- Was the presentation organized?
- Was the presentation educational for the audience?

Game Project

This project is ideally suited for making games that demonstrate information or principles in science and social studies. Students could select specific areas such as whales, general concepts like survival, periods in history like the western movement, social processes like the election process, or identification of specific units like landforms, plants, or vocabulary. The project could also be used to present specific rules and information in language, spelling, or mathematics. In this case, students might make games on such things as homonyms, weekly spelling words, nouns, multiplication facts, or applications of different mathematical functions. While these areas tend not to be as open to creative interpretation as some of the areas of social studies and science, they are very acceptable.

Criteria for evaluation:
- Did the student use time wisely?
- Did the student learn something new as a result of this project?
- Did the student do adequate research?
- Is the game well organized?
- Is the game educational for people playing it?
- Are the rules easy to understand?
- Is the game attractive?
- Is the game fun to play?
- Does the game include elements of both luck and skill?

Learning Center

This project can be used in any subject area but works best when there is definite information or knowledge that is being communicated. Students may wish to select their own topic of interest and create a learning center that would teach other students about this topic. Students could choose such topics as electricity, poetry, history of our community, musical instruments, techniques of building, drawing figures, identification of native plants, or black holes. Advanced students might also make a learning center as an extension of a unit that the entire class has studied. In this case, students who use the learning center would extend or reinforce knowledge that they gained in group instruction. The teacher may also choose to break a unit of study into parts and have each student or group of students create a learning center that would teach other students about that particular aspect of the general topic. An example of this would be learning centers on the Renaissance Period—literature, art, architecture, music, clothing, religion, and science.

Criteria for evaluation:
- Did the student conduct thorough research?
- Did the student make good use of time?
- Did the student select observable objectives?
- Are the activities related to objectives?
- Does the center include a variety of activities?
- Does the center include adequate information sources?
- Are the instructions clear?
- Are the activities easy to understand?
- Is the center attractive?
- Are the activities interesting and appropriate for grade level?
- Is there a wide assortment of alternative activities to account for different learning styles, abilities, and interests?
- Does the center include various media—books, magazines, filmstrips, construction materials, etc.?

Model

Making a model will be particularly popular with students who like doing things with their hands. It is a challenging project, because students not only have to research a topic, but they have to use construction skills to make a three-dimensional model. This application of knowledge can be used in various units of study, though the most common is science. Some ideas for models are:
- turbine, windmill, solar collector, sun dial
- eye, heart, muscles
- house, teepee, castle, igloo, fort
- gold dredge, engine, gears, pulleys
- birds' beaks, animals' feet, homes of burrowing animals
- flowers, root systems, bee hives
- land forms, erosion, sediment layers
- totem poles, baskets, pyramids
- robot, space station, underwater city
- new, improved version of something, an original invention

Criteria for evaluation:
- Did the student make good use of time?
- Is thorough research evident?
- Is the model an accurate representation?
- Is the model carefully constructed?
- Is the model clearly labeled?
- Is the project well organized?
- Is the explanation that accompanies model easy to understand?
- Does the model present a concept or information that is educational for the audience?

Multi-Media Project

A multi-media project has several creative applications for the classroom. In most instances, students will be selecting broad topics as a basis for their research and presentation. The areas that are easiest to adapt to this kind of project are social issues or social happenings, historical perspectives, personal reflections, nature experiences, and information on social problems.

Some possible topics for this type of project might be:
- Our community—what is it?
- A walking tour of_____ (some part of your town, the zoo, etc.)
- Seasons
- Students—what are they thinking, where are they going?
- A look at nature
- The problems associated with aging
- Pollution
- Drug Abuse—some facts
- Happiness is...
- Signs of inner city renewal
- People helping people
- Our historic heroes
- Architecture in our community

- Who are the leaders in our community, and where are they leading us?
- A moment in history reenacted
- How to survive in the woods
- Sports at our school
- Building a future

Criteria for evaluation:
- Is the topic selected appropriate?
- Did the student do thorough research?
- Are the information, concepts and ideas organized?
- Do the pictures add to the quality of the project?
    - clear
    - variety of shots
    - related to the topic
    - present an interesting format
- Does the sound add to the quality of the project?
    - clear
    - variety
    - interesting script
    - reinforces the pictures
- Does the project relate information, tell a story, or create an image?
- Does the project hold the interest of the audience?
- Is overall quality good?

Poster Project

This project could be used purely as an art project, or it could be incorporated with other subjects as a means of communicating information. Some ideas for effective posters include:

- Advertise a book for a book report
- Advertise a product to demonstrate application of advertising techniques
- Safety information
- Announcement of a special event
- Illustration of historical event
- A call to action on a social problem
- Illustration of a scientific or mathematical principle
- Graphic depiction of a poem
- Travel poster for a special city, state, or region
- An informational tool for topics like "Native Wild Flowers," "Historic Places," or "Parts of a Computer System."
- Campaign posters for past presidents
- Anti-pollution posters
- Health information
- Illustrations or advertisements of future means of transportation, future cities, or future technological advances
- Illustration of means of transportation, communication, etc.

Criteria for evaluation:
- Did the student make good use of time?
- Was the topic appropriate for a poster?
- Was the research adequate?
- Does the poster accomplish its purpose?
- Is the headline easy to read and attention-getting?
- Is planning evident?
- Is the design effective and attractive?
- Is the poster unique?
- Is the poster attractive?
- Is the poster attention-getting?

Problem Solution

This project gives students an opportunity to practice the techniques of creative problem solving. The problems they select can be personal problems or problems with world-wide implications. They can be little problems or large problems. More important than the kind of problems students select is for them to exercise creativity as they find solutions. Some ideas for possible problems are:
- How can our class stop loosing so many balls?
- How can we make our classroom quieter?
- How can we solve the parking problem in our town?
- How can we get financing for a new cultural center?
- How can we stop the arms race?
- How can we provide safe environments for endangered animals?
- How can we reduce pollution in our community?
- How can we increase our chances of getting into good colleges?
- How can we prevent child abuse?
- How can we provide more energy from renewable sources?
- How can we educate children about the dangers of drug abuse?
- How can we reduce crime in our city?
- How can we improve the work atmosphere of our classroom?
- How can we improve our country's image with other countries?
- How can we get enough money to go on the field trip?
- How can we increase test scores?
- How can we improve the school bus?
- How can we use leftover egg cartons?
- How can we save paper?
- How can we have more fun playing baseball?

Criteria for evaluation:

- Is the problem correctly defined?
- Did the student collect adequate information?
- Did the student brainstorm many possible solutions?
- Are the criteria relevant to the problem?

- Are the criteria correctly used to select a solution?
- Is the problem solving process correctly applied?
- Is there a unique, original solution?
- Is creativity evident?
- Is the plan of action detailed and precise?
- Is the solution being carried out?

Science Project

The science project is designed to give students an opportunity to explore some field of science and present their findings to the whole class. While this project is left open-ended enough to allow students the opportunity to select a topic for investigation that they are interested in, all projects should demonstrate thorough research, original thinking, and the creation of an experiment, model, collection, or drawings that illustrate this scientific principle. Some potential suggestions for science projects are:

- How does diet affect rats' learning ability? (experiment)
- How does the heart work? (model)
- Spider webs (collection or model)
- How are butterflies born? (experiment with illustrations of various stages)
- What kind of bridge is the most stable? (experiment and model)
- How do rockets work? (model)
- What lives in a tidepool? (collection)
- What is solar energy and how can we use it? (model, demonstration)
- How does a turbine produce energy? (model)
- What are the effects of light on plant growth? (experiment)

Criteria for evaluation:
- Did the student make good use of time?
- Did the student conduct adequate research?
- Was the project question answered?
- Does the project provide a visual display of the scientific information for the audience?
- Is the display attractive and well-organized?
- Is the display educational?
- Is the report well written?

Special Event

A special event is probably the project that demands the most organization, but it is also one of the most enjoyable. It is an opportunity for students to celebrate or demonstrate a happening, event or state of being in a variety of ways. It is an opportunity for "learning by doing." It is different, however, from special-occassion days like "'50s Day" or "Backward Day" in that it is an opportunity for learning. The students who organize this special event should gain considerable knowledge about the specific topic through their research. The students (or parents) who take part in this special event should also come away with increased knowledge or heightened appreciation. There are a wide variety of educational experiences that would lend themselves to this type of activity. Possible ideas are:
- Olympic night
- Elizabethan day
- Renaissance fair
- Science all around you day
- Job fair
- Handicap awareness day
- Obon festival
- Personal growth day
- Favorite author day
- Favorite fairy tale character day
- Appreciation days
- Cultural heritage day
- Meeting of the minds (inventors, explorers, scientists, etc.)
- Cinco de Mayo
- Our community
- Arts awareness day
- Step back in history day
- Energy awareness day
- A day in the life of _____ (famous person or historical figure)
- Gold rush reenactment
- Simulation of caste system.

Criteria for evaluation:
- Was the topic appropriate for this project?
- Was the theme accurately carried out?
- Did everything happen as planned?
- Was the event well-organized?
- Was adequate research conducted?
- Did the activities involve all participants actively?
- Did people enjoy the event?
- Was it a learning experience for participants?
- Were there a variety of activities?

Speech/Oral Report

A speech or oral report can be used in a variety of learning situations. You may assign a speech as a means of presenting information from a research project. The topic of research may be something that the student has chosen or a topic that you have assigned. Some students find it easier to organize their thoughts for an oral presentation than to make a written presentation, so unless your objective is a written research paper, you may want to give students the choice of how they will present their research. Speeches are not, however, solely for reporting information. The topic of the speech could be personal (*What I Am Most Proud Of*, *My Goals for the Future*, or *How I Got to Be This Way*) or controversial (*Why Do We Need Nuclear Weapons?*, *Proposed Changes for Our School*, or *Why a Woman Would Make a Better President*). Speeches can inform, entertain, persuade and inspire. If your objective is to have students develop a particular line of reasoning as well as practice speech skills, your assignment will be different than if you merely want them to research a topic and orally communicate the information.

Criteria for evaluation:
- Did the student make wise use of time?
- Is the topic interesting?
- Does the student show knowledge of the subject?
- Does the speech show good organization?
- Does delivery show good techniques?
  - diction
  - voice projection/volume
  - eye contact
  - variety in pitch, tone, and tempo
  - body language
- Is the speech interesting and easy to understand?
- Are the visual aids effective and easy to see?
- Has the student provided evidence of research?

Survey Project

The survey project could be used as a project by itself where the goal is to introduce students to the techniques of taking a survey. It is most effective, however, when it is a part of some unit of study—either one that is assigned by the instructor or one that is selected by the student. In the latter case, students use the results of their surveys as information that they can incorporate into their study units. When students are studying contemporary issues or problems they will find many topics that would be appropriate for a survey. Such topics include:

- How many hours of television do students watch each week?
- Should welfare recipients be required to work?
- Should our school district ban certain books from literature classes?

- Should our country have a woman president?
- Should the government increase funding for education? Cancer research? Defense? Welfare?
- Should records include a rating similar to movies?
- What do people want for our community in the future?
- What are the biggest problems facing students today?
- What books are favorites with students our age?
- What skills will be most valuable to students when they enter the workforce?

Criteria for evaluation:
- Is the topic appropriate for a survey?
- Is the sample carefully selected?
- Are the questions carefully worded to avoid bias?
- Are the questions selected to accurately reflect the topic?
- Is the sample representative of the general population?
- Are there several questions for each item?
- Is the data accurately collected?
- Is the graphic representation clear?
- Are conclusions valid?
- Is the summary and presentation easy to understand?

- Is pollution a curable problem?
- Bermuda Triangle—fact or fiction?
- What happened to the dinosaurs?

Criteria for evaluation:
- Did the student make wise use of time?
- Was the topic question thought-provoking?
- Did the student do adequate research?
- Is the information well-organized?
- Does the student include original ideas?
- Is the report easy to read and interesting?
- Does the report contain a complete bibliography?
- Is the spelling correct?
- Does the student use proper grammar?

Written Report

Written reports are probably the most common product in schools. While they are not usually the most interesting (either for students who have to write them or for teachers who have to grade them), they do provide valuable experience in organizing ones' thoughts for written communication. Teachers usually need no help in finding learning situations that are appropriate for written reports. Practically every subject has some body of information that would lend itself to a written report. What is important, though, is that students do more than copy out of reference books. Research topics should be posed that call for original thinking. Examples of topics that would elicit this combination of research and thinking are:
- What is the future of our community?
- What, if anything, is more precious than gold? Why?
- How were the 1950s different from the 1960s? Which decade would you have liked to live through?
- What ethical and medical considerations surround medical experimentation on animals?
- Do we need a king as well as a president?
- Women: Where have we been and where are we going?
- How is education related to economics? politics? values?
- What are the common values of the people in our community?

Research Record

Name _____

Topic _____

Resource _____

_____

_____

Facts and Concepts

_____
_____
_____
_____
_____
_____
_____
_____
_____
_____
_____
_____
_____
_____
_____
_____
_____
_____
_____
_____
_____
_____
_____
_____

Put an * by the facts or concepts you think are the most important or most useful in your project.

Evaluation

Name_____

Topic _____

Project _____

Rate each item according to the following scale:

4 = excellent
3 = very good
2 = satisfactory
1 = needs improvement
0 = not observed

criteria	student	teacher
1. _____		
2. _____		
3. _____		
4. _____		
5. _____		
6. _____		
7. _____		
8. _____		
9. _____		
10. _____		

What do you think is the best thing about this presentation?

Student _____

_____

Teacher _____

_____

What do you think could be improved?

Student _____

_____

Teacher _____

_____

Did you learn something as a result of this project?

_____

_____

17

Book Project

For this project, you will be writing a book. As you know from your own reading, books can cover a wide variety of subjects and can be produced in several different formats. Once you have looked at several different kinds of books and decided what kind of book you want to write, you will need both organization and creativity to take you through to the finished product. This assignment sheet shows you what you need to do to create an attractive book. Check off each step as you complete it.

☐ **1. Look around**
   Look at books in your library and personal collection. Notice all the different kinds of books. Start looking around you for every-day experiences that might make a good basis for a book. Take notes on anything and everything that you think might relate to this project.

☐ **2. Decide on format and subject matter**
   Decide whether you will write a fiction or non-fiction book. Will your book be for younger children, older children, or general reference? What form will it be—short story, novel, poetry collection, how-to-do-it book, color book, work book, information book, picture book, educational book, journal, letters, or some other unique format? Briefly describe the kind of book you want to write.

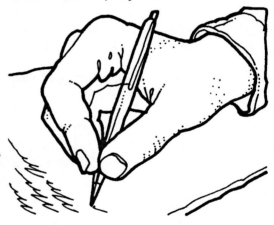

   I think my book will be _____

   _____

☐ **3. Research**
   Authors usually write about things they are familiar with. To become more familiar with your topic, you will need to get information about the topic, setting, history, characters, or events. Collect any information that you think will make your book more interesting. Even if you are writing a fictional story, facts will make your story more interesting and believable. Besides reading books and magazine articles, also talk to people, visit museums or special exhibits, look up old records, or read magazine articles. Keep a record of your research by recording the information on the Research Record sheets or on note cards.

19

☐ **4. Analyze reader**
Decide what kind of readers you are writing for—what age group, what reading level, and what interests. Decide what readers will want to get out of the writing. Will they be reading for facts and information, mental pictures, humor, entertainment, or some other reason? If you are writing for younger children, make sure they will be able to relate to and find interest in your topic.

Description of the intended reader _____

_____

☐ **5. Plan your book**
Briefly write out the contents of your book and the proposed order by making a list of events or an outline.

If you are writing a **story**, plot the main events. List the main characters and describe what they are like. Remember that every plot must feature a problem to solve and a solution. The problem could be nature, another character, a personal characteristic, or some other obstacle. A story without a problem could be very boring for most readers.

If you are writing an **information book**, outline how you will present the main concepts.

☐ **6. Write the first draft**
Refer to the guidelines for writing books. Then write the first copy of your book. Double space so you can easily make corrections later.

☐ **7. Proofread**
Proofread for spelling, content, and grammar. Read your book out loud. Ask a friend or parent to read it and give constructive criticisms. Look critically for ways you could improve what you have written. Make any necessary changes.

☐ **8. Plan book format**
Calculate how many pages your book will have. Plan out what print and what pictures or illustrations will be on each page. Remember that if you are writing for younger children, you will need to have many more illustrations than if you were writing for older people. You might also want to include things they can touch and do as well as things they can see. Decide on what kind of binding you will use. Make a layout for each page.

20

☐ **9. Write final draft**
Write or type your book as you want it to be in its final form. Leave room for illustrations.

☐ **10. Add illustrations**
Carefully draw any pictures, charts, or diagrams.

☐ **11. Make a cover for your book**
Your cover should include an attractive illustration that will interest readers in reading your book, a catchy title, and your name.

☐ **12. Bind book**

☐ **13. Share your book**

☐ **14. Evaluate**
Use the evaluation form provided by your teacher to evaluate your work on this project.

☐ **15. Application**
1. Write a brief description (no more than 75 words) of your book suitable for a catalog that sells books. Entice the reader to buy your book. Include title, author, pages, and price.

2. You have decided that your book is good enough to be published. Write a letter to a publisher that is a brief, but convincing, appeal to look at your manuscript. Point out why your book is different from others on the market or is a needed addition to existing literature. Establish yourself as an authority.

Guidelines for Writing a Book

Stories:

- Develop an interesting, attention-getting introduction that will make the reader want to read more.

- Describe characters, time, and setting either directly or indirectly.

- Use both narrative (describing characters, setting and actions from the author's perspective) and dialogue (what the characters say).

- Include a problem and a solution to the problem in your plot.

- Build to a climax and then find a quick solution.

- Write the story either in the first person (as told by one of the characters) or the third person (the author describes what is happening). Do not switch back and forth between the two styles.

- Use action words.

- Replace common words with more descriptive words.

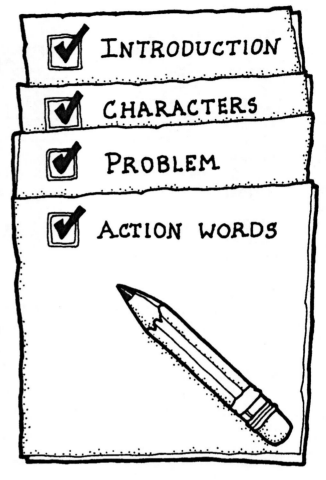

✓ INTRODUCTION
✓ CHARACTERS
✓ PROBLEM
✓ ACTION WORDS

Factual books:

- Try to make your topic as interesting as possible.

- Include interesting or surprising facts.

- Draw people into the topic by asking questions like "What if?" or "Have you ever thought what would happen?"

- Use words and phrases that paint a picture.

- Back up generalizations with specific information and facts.

- Develop one idea thoroughly before moving onto the next.

- Proceed in an orderly fashion, relating one idea to the next one. Do not jump around.

Debate Project

A debate is a special kind of persuasive speech. The object of a debate is to win the debate by presenting the best, most convincing arguments. For this project you will be working with other people on a debate team. Your team will take one side of an issue or question, and try to prove to the audience that your view or your side is the most convincing. The winning team will be determined by the logic of the arguments, the facts to back up the arguments, and a convincing manner of delivery.

This project will take a lot of preparation and research, but the resulting debate should prove to be exciting. This assignment sheet shows you the basic steps that you will have to follow to prepare for and deliver a convincing debate argument. Check off each step as you complete it.

☐ **1. Choose debating team**
A debating team usually consists of two debaters and an alternative debater. During a debate the two debaters do all of the speaking, while the alternate takes notes and gives the debaters advice. The alternate is also familiar with all of the information so he/she can fill in for one of the debaters or take over the position of debater should the debate be staged more than once. Your team may or may mot have an alternate debater. Check with your teacher so see how many people will be on your debating team. Select team members.

Members of the debating team are _____

_____

☐ **2. Select resolution**
The topic of the debate is stated in the form of a **resolution** or **proposition**. It is usually stated, "Resolved that..." Check with your teacher for a debate assignment or for a list of approved resolutions.

Debate resolution: _____

_____

☐ **3. Select positions**
One team of debaters will argue for the resolution. This team will take the **affirmative** side. The affirmative argues that the resolution should be adopted or that it is advantageous to society. The other team of debaters will argue against the resolution. This team will take the **negative** side. The negative side tries to defend the present condition and prevent the adoption of the resolution.

Affirmative team _____

Resolution stated in the affirmative: _____

_____

Negative team _____

Resolution stated in the negative: _____

_____

☐ **4. Research**
You will need to gather as much up-to-date information on your topic as possible. You will need facts, figures, and opinions of experts in the field. You may be able to find books that deal with your topic, but to get the most current information, you should check newspapers, magazines, pamphlets, and other reference books. You should also try to get information from people who are experts in the field. Keep track of your information by writing it on note cards—one idea or one fact per card. Record where you got the information. If you need to quote someone's opinion, record the quotation exactly as well as the name of the person, his/her qualifications, and the date.

I have completed research using the following sources of information:

_____

_____

_____

_____

_____

_____

☐ **5. Organize research**
Your goal in a debate is to prove your claim. Proof is always achieved by a combination of evidence and reasoning. It is not enough to merely present lots of facts and figures. You must combine this evidence with logical reasons for supporting your claim. But no matter how brilliant your arguments and how vital your evidence, your arguments will be lost if they are not presented in an organized fashion.

With your debate partner, plan your reasoning and organize your information. Your presentation should have a few major points and several minor points that support or develop the major points. Facts, figures and quotes support major and minor points. Once you have decided on the main points divide the quotes, facts, and figures into major points and minor points. Remember that while material may be divided among team members, each person on the team should be familiar with all the information so he/she can use it to dispute claims made by the other team. Decide on the most logical order to present information to the audience.

☐ **6. Write presentation**
In a debate, you cannot read your speech. In fact, the first person to speak is the only person who has a totally prepared presentation. You can, however, have notes that contain all of the information you wish to present in an organized fashion. Write your arguments on note cards, including all facts, figures, and quotes that you will need to substantiate your main points.

☐ **7. Prepare refutation**
In a debate you should present a convincing argument, and counter the arguments of the opposing side. Be prepared to deny or disprove anything that the opposition presents. To do this, you must try to think of all the arguments your opposition is likely to make and collect data or information to refute them.

List all of the arguments you think the opposing team will present. Put one argument on the top of a piece of paper or note card. Go back to the library and search for information that will counter each argument. Write the information or facts on each piece of paper under the appropriate argument.

☐ **8. Practice**
Go through your debate with your partner. Review who will present each argument. Make sure that all issues and arguments are covered. Practice presenting your arguments in an organized and convincing manner. Give each other constructive criticism on delivery.

☐ **9. Debate**
When you debate, you will follow all the same rules for delivering a speech. One other thing that you will have to do, though, is to listen carefully to what the other team is saying and make note of any arguments that you can refute.

Your debate will have a chairperson who will call the debate to order, announce the resolution, introduce the teams, start the debate by calling on the affirmative side to speak, and time each speech.

25

Debates follow a formal routine. Both teams are seated at a table facing the audience. The affirmative side sits on one side of the chairperson. The negative team sits on the other side. The teams speak in the following order:

Constructive - This is a time when each team builds or constructs a case by introducing arguments and supporting evidence. The speaking order is:

1. *First affirmative* - states the resolution, defines terms, and presents justification for accepting the resolution. (10 minutes)
2. *First negative* - states any objections to definitions of terms, presents opening arguments to refute the resolution, lays out major issues of the negative side. (10 minutes)
3. *Second affirmative* - continues the affirmative argument by reestablishing the affirmative position and extending affirmative arguments. (10 minutes)
4. *Second negative* - continues the negative argument, reviewing negative issues. (10 minutes)

Rebuttal - This is the time for each team to attack or defend the points that were introduced in the constructive phase. No new arguments are introduced at this point, but teams can give additional evidence and extend arguments that were already presented. The speaking order is:

1. *First negative* - continues negative arguments, extending and developing arguments that have already been introduced and refutes affirmative position. (5 minutes)
2. *First affirmative* - responds to negative arguments. (5 minutes)
3. *Second negative* - presents an overview of the strongest points and best arguments that refute the resolution. (5 minutes)
4. *Second affirmative* - presents an overview of the strongest points in favor of the resolution and the arguments that best refute the negative position.(5 minutes)

☐ **10. Judging**
   The audience or a team of judges will judge the team that has made the best presentation.

☐ **11. Evaluation**
   Use the evaluation form provided by your teacher to evaluate your work on this project.

☐ **12. Application**
   1. If you put this resolution to a vote, how do you think the majority of people would vote? Would it make any difference if the voter was a woman or a man, young or old, living in our country or living in another country, employed or unemployed? What other factors might make a difference in how someone voted?
   2. Are you convinced that your side or position in this debate is right? Why? Who might agree with you? Who might disagree?
   3. Is there a compromise position? What might it be?

Demonstration Project

What is something that you know how to do that you could demonstrate to other people? Once you think about it, there are probably many things that you could be considered an expert (or at least a semi-expert) on. This is you chance to share your expertise. In this project, you will be selecting something that you know how to do and showing other people in your group how to do it.

As with other projects, you will need to organize your project so that your presentation is concise and easy to understand. Your goal is to educate your audience. To do this, you must carefully plan what you will say and do. This assignment sheet shows you everything you need to do to successfully complete this project. Check off each step as you complete it.

☐ **1. List what you know**
Make a list of all the things that you know how to do that you could share with your class.

_____   _____
_____   _____
_____   _____
_____   _____

☐ **2. Choose a topic**
From the list you just made, choose something that you would feel comfortable demonstrating and that other people would find interesting.

I will demonstrate _____

☐ **3. List steps**
Make a list of all of the main steps or procedures that are involved in doing this thing.

_____
_____
_____
_____
_____
_____
_____
_____

27

☐ **4. List materials**
   Make a list of the materials, equipment, or visual aids that you will need.

   _____

   _____

   _____

   _____

   _____

☐ **5. Assess what you know**
   Make a list of other information you might need in addition to what you already know. Consider facts, history, or stories that would make your presentation more entertaining and informative.

   Other information I need:

   _____

   _____

   _____

   _____

   _____

   Where I could find this information:

   _____

   _____

   _____

☐ **6. Research**
   Gather information on your topic. Take notes from your research and keep accurate records of your sources of information.

   I have completed research using these sources of information:

   _____

   _____

   _____

   _____

☐ **7. Make an outline**
   Make an outline that combines the steps you listed in number three with new information you collected from your research.

☐ **8. Prepare speech notes**
   Either use a detailed outline or note cards to list all of the steps you will demonstrate and everything you will say. Print your notes in large letters, so they are easy to read. Make note of when you will show materials or visual aids. If you use note cards, number them to indicate the correct order.

☐ **9. Organize materials**
   Get together everything you will need for your demonstration. Make sure everything works and that props are big enough for everyone to see. Organize materials so that they are available when you need them.

☐ **10. Practice**
   Go through your demonstration in front of a mirror, with a tape recorder, or for a friend. Practice several times, if necessary. Make any changes that will improve your demonstration.

☐ **11. Make presentation**

☐ **12. Evaluate**
   Use the evaluation form provided by your teacher to evaluate your work on this project.

☐ **13. Application**
   You have just won a grant to "take your show on the road." You will spend the next three months presenting your demonstration to audiences in various cities around the country. Design a poster that will serve as an announcement for your demonstration.

Display Project

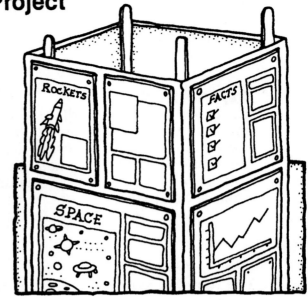

In this project, you will communicating ideas and information to other people in a graphic form. You will be researching a topic and then sharing the results of your research on the three-dimensional faces of an **idea cube**, on a **bulletin board**, or in a **display**. A bulletin board is a large two-dimensional display such as the ones you have lining the walls of your classroom. An idea cube is like a three-dimensional bulletin board. A display can include the use of posters or bulletin boards to display information but usually also includes objects for people to view or observe.

This project will give you the opportunity to communicate ideas in a variety of ways. If it sounds like fun, it is! If it sounds like you will have to be a creative thinker, you're right! This assignment sheet shows you everything you need to do to construct an attractive, informative display. Check off each step as you complete it.

☐ **1. Decide on topic**
Choose a topic that you think will be interesting to you and to other people.

My topic is_____

☐ **2. Assess present knowledge**

_____I already know a lot about this topic, but I could learn more.
_____I already know a little about this topic.
_____I don't know very much about this topic.

☐ **3. Research**
Use _____ different references to gather information on your topic. Take notes from your research. Keep records of your sources of information, so you will have all of the facts you need to complete an accurate bibliography and to recheck sources if needed. Consider using some of these different sources of information:

- magazine articles, pamphlets, newspapers, and reports
- reference books
- field trip
- books
- movies, slides, filmstrips, videos, or television specials

- charts, tables, graphs, diagrams, collections, or maps
- interview an authority
- experiment or survey
- guided observations
- conferences, seminars, or performances

30

I have completed research using these sources of information:

_____

_____

_____

_____

☐ **4. Select information**
Select the information that you think is the most important or most interesting. Put an * by the facts and concepts that you think are the most important.

☐ **5. Decide on presentation**
Brainstorm a list of several different ways that this information could be presented. The ideas you list should show variety and be graphic in nature. Your goal is to create an attention-getting display. A box or bulletin board covered with a written report would not attract attention. Instead, you want attract the viewers' attention and capture their interest in learning more about this topic.
Consider using some of these techniques:
- *Graphs, maps, short written summaries, pictures or illustrations, charts, artifacts, mottoes or sayings, models, letters, crafts, quizzes, samples, or descriptive headlines.*

My project will include:
a_____ of _____
a_____ saying _____
a_____ of _____

_____

_____

_____

_____

_____

☐ **6. Prepare objects for display**
Collect or make all of the things that you will be putting in your display. Remember that every item should present an idea or fact about your topic. Make everything big, bold, and colorful. Consider cutting out, tracing, drawing pictures, words, graphic representations, or illustrations. Clearly label everything so people can tell what it is.

31

□ **7. Prepare display surface**
Cover box with paper if you are making an idea box. For a bulletin board, choose a suitable background and put it on the board. For a display, make a backdrop out of cardboard that has been painted or covered with paper.

□ **8. Mount objects on display surface**
Glue or tack all of your words, pictures, graphs, etc. on the surface of the display. If you have made a model or have some three-dimensional items that cannot be glued to the bulletin board or box, place them beside your display.

Your finished product should have the following characteristics:
- is covered (in the case of the box, on five surfaces)
- main headlines or titles are visible from a distance
- communicates an idea or information
- has a variety of things for people to look at, read, or do
- has a combination of presentation techniques
- creates interest in the topic

□ **9. Present your project**

□ **10. Evaluation**
Use the evaluation form provided by your teacher to evaluate your work on this project.

□ **11. Application**
What information on this display is most likely to change in the next ten years? What effects will this have?

Experiment

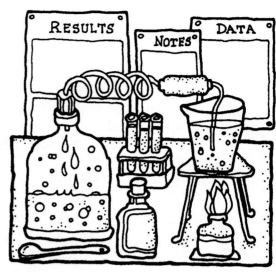

An experiment is a test or trial that you do in order to discover something that you do not yet know or to demonstrate something that is known. When you try an experiment, you must limit the number of things, or variables, that you are testing. You also must have some means of carefully observing, measuring, and recording the results of the experiment. Many experiments must be performed several times, each time collecting data from the experiment and comparing it to data from other trials.

In this project, you will be conducting an experiment, recording the results, and drawing conclusions based on the data you collected. This assignment sheet shows each step that you must follow. Check off each step as you complete it.

☐ **1. Choose a topic**
Think of several possible topics. Then choose the particular topic that you think would be most interesting to investigate.

My topic of study will be _____

☐ **2. Assess present knowledge**

_____I know a lot about this subject, but I could learn more.
_____I know some things about this subject.
_____I don't know very much about this topic.

☐ **3. Ask questions**
Ask several questions that could be answered by performing an experiment.

_____

_____

_____

_____

_____

33

☐ **4. Select a question**
   Select one question that you would like to use for an experiment.

   _____

☐ **5. Design experiment**
   Decide what you will do to find the answer to your question. To do this, first describe your **procedure**—what you will do, what you will observe, what you will measure, and how you will record the results of your experiment. Then state a **hypothesis**, or what you think will happen.

   Procedure:
   What I will do:

   _____
   _____
   _____
   _____

   What I will observe:

   _____
   _____

   What I will measure:

   _____
   _____

   How I will record the results of the experiment:

   _____
   _____
   _____

   Hypothesis (what I think will happen):

   _____
   _____
   _____

☐ **6. Gather materials**

Make a list of all the materials you will need. Check off each item when you get it.

_____

_____

_____

_____

_____

_____

_____

_____

_____

_____

☐ **7. Perform the experiment**

Carefully perform the experiment and record the results.

☐ **8. Organize your data**

Put the results of your experiment in some form that will make them easy to compare. You might consider making a graph, chart, or a table.

☐ **9. Analyze the results**

Carefully look at the data you have collected. Based on this information, what conclusions can you make?

Based on this information I can conclude _____

_____

_____

_____

_____

☐ **10. Research**
Look for information that would back up or explain the results of your experiment. Use _____ different sources of information. Take notes from your research and keep careful records of your sources of information.

I completed research using these sources of information:

_____

_____

_____

_____

_____

_____

_____

☐ **11. Write report**
Write a brief report that summarizes the information you gathered in your research.

☐ **12. Share your experiment**
Demonstrate your experiment for your class. If you cannot perform the entire experiment, explain what you did and show the results. Based on the results of the experiment and the research you did, explain what happened and why it happened.

☐ **13. Evaluation**
Complete the evaluation form provided by your teacher.

☐ **14. Application**
1. What other variables could be tested?
2. How can this information be used?

36

Experiment Record Sheet

Name_____

Experiment question _____

Hypothesis (what you think will happen) _____
_____

Drawing of experiment

Procedure _____
_____
_____

Results _____
_____
_____
_____
_____
_____
_____
_____

Conclusion _____
_____
_____
_____

Record the results of the experiment on a separate graph, chart, or table and attach it to this sheet.

Game Project

There are many kinds of games—card games, board games, video games, group games, solitary games, games of skill, and games of luck. While many games are played solely for enjoyment, many other games are designed to test the players' knowledge or ability to think. Games have been a part of our lives for hundreds of years. Games have been used to entertain, to challenge, and to teach.

For this project, you will be choosing a topic in the area that interests you. You will then be doing research to learn more about this topic. After you have done your research, you will make a game that will teach players some of the things you have learned.

This assignment sheet shows you everything you will have to do in order to make an educational and entertaining game. Check off each step as you complete it.

☐ **1. Choose a topic**
Think about several different topics. Then choose the one topic that interests you and also has information or concepts that could easily be made into a game.

The topic I want to study is _____

☐ **2. Assess present knowledge**

_____I know a lot about this topic, but I could learn more.
_____I know some things about this topic.
_____I don't know very much about this topic.

☐ **3. Research**
Use _____ different references to gather information on your topic. Take notes from your research. Keep records of your sources of information, so you will have all of the facts you need to complete an accurate bibliography and to recheck sources if needed. Consider using some of these different sources of information:

- magazine articles, pamphlets, newspapers, and reports
- reference books (encyclopedias, etc.)
- field trip
- books
- movies, slides, filmstrips, videos, or television specials

- charts, tables, graphs, diagrams, collections, or maps
- interview an authority
- experiment or survey
- guided observations
- conferences, seminars, or performances
- other _____

I have completed research using these sources of information:

_____

_____

_____

☐ **4. Decide on concepts or information**
What concepts or information will be presented in the game? What will players learn about or be able to do after playing this game? What are the concepts to be understood, the skills to be mastered, or the facts to be learned?

By playing this game players will _____

_____

☐ **5. Decide on players' roles**
What do the players represent? What part do they play in the game? How many players can play at one time? What do players do? What things are mechanized (part of the game or chance) and what things are human factors?

_____

_____

☐ **6. Decide on the players' goal**
Most games use one of three strategies — buying, capturing, or racing. Players are usually trying to buy the most resources, capture something like territory, resources, or enemy pieces, racing to get to the goal first, or some combination of strategies.

What are the players of your game trying to do? Are they trying to gain power or wealth? Are they trying to get to the end? Are they trying to stay alive? Or are they trying gain possession of the most resources?

_____

_____

☐ **7. Decide on the players' resources**
What things will the players be trying to get? Do they want the most money, power, information, right answers, chips, power pellets, matches, or pairs? How will these things be represented in the game?

_____

_____

_____

☐ **8. Decide on the sequence**
How do players take turns? What is the sequence of steps? For example, do you roll dice, move your marker and draw a card? How can you include hazards or lucky breaks to make the game more interesting?

_____

_____

_____

☐ **9. Decide on scoring**
How do the resources relate to scoring? How is scoring related to how well the players achieve the objective of the game?

_____

_____

_____

☐ **10. Decide on the rules**
Write rules that are concise and easy to understand.

_____

_____

_____

_____

_____

Continue on another piece of paper if you need more room.

☐ **11. Decide on the form**
What form will your game be—board game, paper and pencil, computer, cards, simulation, or some other form?

_____

□ **12. Give your game a unique name**
The name of my game is _____

□ **13. Make a basic model**
Make a model of your game and test it out with some friends.

□ **14. Make any necessary changes**

□ **15. Gather materials**
Make a list of materials you will need. Check off each item as you get it.

_____ _____
_____ _____
_____
_____
_____
_____
_____
_____
_____ _____
_____ _____

□ **16. Make the game**
Make the final version of your game. Make it attractive and durable. Include a list of rules, all necessary playing pieces, and a way to store all the parts of your game when it is not being used.

□ **17. Play the game**

□ **18. Evaluation**
Complete the evaluation form provided by your teacher.

□ **19. Application**
How would you market this game? Write a short advertisement that would convince someone to buy your game.

Learning Center

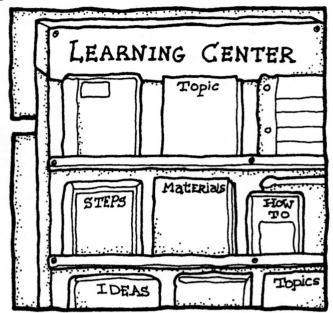

A learning center is a place where students can work individually or in a small group to learn something new and to practice skills they have already been taught. A learning center can take many different forms. Regardless of its form, a learning center will always give learners everything they need to learn and to practice the information that is presented. Learning centers usually include the following:
- information about the topic
- activities and instructions
- a list of things to do
- materials and/or equipment

In this project, you will be creating a learning center for other students. You will choose a study topic and then plan learning activities that will help students understand certain information about this topic. This assignment sheet shows you each step you must follow. Check off each step as you complete it.

☐ **1. Choose a topic**
My topic will be _____

☐ **2. Choose an age group**
My learning center will be for _____

☐ **3. Assess present knowledge**

_____I know a lot about this subject, but I could learn more.
_____I know some things about this subject.
_____I know very little about this subject.

☐ **4. Research**
Use _____ different references to gather information on your topic. Take notes from your research. Keep records of your sources of information, so you will have all of the facts you need to complete an accurate bibliography and to recheck sources if needed. Consider using some of these different sources of information:

- magazine articles, pamphlets, newspapers, and reports
- reference books (encyclopedias, etc.)
- field trip
- books
- movies, slides, filmstrips, videos, or television specials

- charts, tables, graphs, diagrams, collections, or maps
- interview an authority on the subject
- experiment or survey
- guided observations
- conferences, seminars, or performances

I have completed research using these sources of information:

_____

_____

_____

_____

☐ **5. Select information**
Choose what information you will present in the learning center by marking the most important information from your notes.

☐ **6. Write objectives**
Objectives are statements of what you want the people using your learning center to accomplish—what they will learn or what they will be able to do as a result of doing the activities in your learning center. **Objectives must be observable.** This means that you will be able to tell whether someone has learned the material that you have presented by observing whether they are able to correctly do some thing. This means that you will use words like *identify, match, group, arrange, take apart, solve, describe, connect, judge, construct, dissect, put in sequence, diagram, put in order, write, illustrate, define, invent, list, choose, write, or draw* in your objectives.
For example:
- Students will be able to identify the subject of a sentence by <u>drawing a line</u> under the subject.
- Students will be able to <u>list</u> the main organs of the body.
- Students will be able to <u>correctly add</u> a column of five single-digit numbers.

Write _____ objectives for your learning center by completing this sentence:

As a result of doing the activities in this center, students will be able to...

_____

_____

_____

_____

☐ **7. Choose sources of information**
Your center must supply students with information as well as opportunities to do activities. There are many different ways of communicating information. You could supply books, magazines, and reports. You could also use maps, charts, filmstrips, tape recordings and games in your center. Choose sources of information that are interesting, geared to the level of the students that will use the center, and easy to use. Remember that students may only spend a short amount of time at your center. You do not want them to spend all of that time reading a lengthy report.

I will provide information in the form of:

_____
_____
_____
_____

☐ **8. Decide on activities**
Decide on what activities you will put in your learning center to support each objective and communicate information. You may include things like games, worksheets, puzzles, things to examine, things to categorize, charts to complete, things to locate on maps, task cards, experiments, or other creative things to do. Remember to include a variety of things to do.

My learning center will include these activities:

_____
_____
_____
_____
_____
_____
_____
_____
_____
_____

☐ **9. Gather materials**

Make a list of all of the materials you will need. You will need to collect information (magazine articles, reports, charts, books, etc.) to put in the learning center as well as materials to make the activities. Check off each item when you get it.

_____   _____

_____   _____

_____

_____

_____

_____

_____

_____

_____

☐ **10. Make activities**

Make the games, activities, worksheets and task cards. Activities should be interesting, attractive, and easy to understand. Find some way to store and display each activity—folders, pockets, boxes, rings, posters, etc. Be creative!

☐ **11. Write instructions**

Write clear, concise instructions that tell students what they are supposed to do at this learning center. If activities need to be completed in a specific sequence, include this in your instructions. Write instructions for each activity.

☐ **12. Make learning center**

Put all of the activities in your learning center together on a piece of poster board, in a box, on a table, in a corner, on a bulletin board, or in some other creative form. Your center should include the following things:

- an attention-getting sign and picture
- a list of things to do at the center
- information about the topic
- activities and instructions
- materials and equipment (everything that is needed to complete the activities)
- a place to hand in work or to record which activities each person has completed

45

☐ **13. Try out**
Use your learning center with students in your classroom or from another classroom.

☐ **14. Evaluate**
Use the evaluation form provided by your teacher to evaluate this project.

☐ **15. Application**
1. How important is it to know the information presented in your learning center? Give two examples of when someone would use this information.

2. If you were writing a textbook for school children about this topic, what would the chapter title and five subheadings be?

Model Project

Models are useful for seeing something that is not usually visible because it is too big (solar system), too small (molecules), no longer in existence (historical village), hidden from normal vision (heart), or not yet in existence (city of the future).

With this project, you will be making a model, or a representation of something real. Models are usually three-dimensional. If they are smaller or larger than the actual size, they are usually made "to scale." Your model will show people how something works, what it looks like, or what its important features are.

This project calls for a combination of research and accurate construction. This assignment sheet shows you everything you need to do to make an accurate model. Check off each step as you complete it.

☐ **1. Select your subject area**
If your teacher has not assigned a project in a specific subject, select the general area of study that you would like to explore.

My general topic of study will be _____

☐ **2. Assess present knowledge**
_____I know a lot about this topic, but I could learn more.
_____I know some things about this topic.
_____I don't know very much about this topic.

☐ **3. Decide on model**
Select the specific thing for which you will make a model.

I will make a model of _____

☐ **4. Research**
Use _____ different references to gather information on your topic. Look for information that will help you make an accurate model and provide specific facts and information about the model. Take notes from your research. Keep records of your sources of information. Look for answers to some of these questions:

- Where is it located or used?
- What is its function?
- How does it work?
- What special care does it need?
- When was it used?

- What are its general characteristics?
- What does it look like?
- How big is it?
- What are some specific variations?
- What other important information would be interesting?

I have completed research using these sources of information:

_____

_____

_____

_____

_____

☐ **5. Make a drawing**
Make a drawing of what your model will be like. Decide on the scale—how many feet or miles will be represented by each inch in the model.

☐ **6. Get technical assistance**
If making your model will involve doing something that you have never done before, you may need to find out how to do it. Contact people who can show you how to do this or refer to how-to-do-it books that explain what you need to do.

☐ **7. Make a list of materials**
Make a list of all of the materials you will need. Check off each item as you get it.

_____

_____

_____

_____

_____

_____

_____

☐ **8. Make model**
Make your model. Be sure to construct it carefully and with accuracy. It is important that your model look as much like the real thing as possible. This will happen only if you carefully plan out the project and exercise great care in carrying out that plan.

☐ **9. Label parts**
Label all important parts of your model. Write clearly so people can easily read the labels.

NOSE · PILOT→ · TAIL→ · Z916 · ←WHEEL · Future PLANE · WING · ENGINE

☐ **10. Write explanation**
Write an explanation to accompany your model that explains how it works, what the important parts are, and any other important information from your research.

☐ **11. Present model**
When you present your model to your class, be ready to explain what it is, how it works, why it is important, and what its important parts are. Include information in your presentation that the audience will find useful and thought-provoking.

☐ **12. Evaluate**
Use the evaluation form provided by your teacher to evaluate your work on this project.

☐ **13. Application**
How could it be improved?
What could it be used for besides its usual function?
What are some things we do **not** know about it?

Multi-Media Project

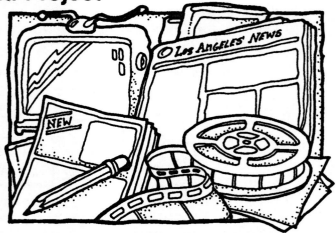

Media refers to a means of communicating ideas to a large number of people. It usually includes radio, television, movies, newspapers, video, and magazines. A multi-media project is one that involves more than just one form of communication. It is usually a combination of pictures and sound—like a movie with a sound track, a video tape with sound, or a slide show with accompanying dialogue on a tape recorder.

For this project you will be producing a multi-media presentation. It will take creative thinking to select a topic that is well-suited to this kind of presentation. It will then take careful planning to transform this idea into an interesting, informative, and visually-appealing multi-media presentation. This assignment sheet shows you everything you need to do to assemble a multi-media project. Check off each step as you complete it.

☐ **1. Select a topic**
Choose a topic that is appropriate subject matter for a film, video tape, or slide presentation. Your topic should be something you find fascinating and something that will be interesting and informative for other people.

My topic will be _____

☐ **2. Assess what you know**

_____I know a lot about this subject, but I could learn more.
_____I know some things about this subject.
_____I don't know very much about this subject.

☐ **3. Brainstorm ideas**

Make a long list of different ways you could approach this subject. List different points of view, people or organizations that are involved, questions you could ask, and subtopics of your general topic. Consider all possible formats—interview, documentary, educational demonstration, quiz or game shows, variety show, historic reenactment, informative review, man-on-the-street interview, fictional play, panel discussion, or nature experience.

_____
_____
_____
_____
_____

Continue listing ideas on the back of this piece of paper.

☐ **4. Narrow the focus**
Choose the best idea(s) from the list you brainstormed. This will be the focus and format of your project.

☐ **5. Research**
All documentary filmmakers do extensive research on the topic they are making a movie or video about. Though your final product will be a series of pictures, you will need to collect background information and facts to present with these pictures.

Use _____ different references to gather information on your topic. Record notes from your research. Keep records of your sources of information, so you will have all of the facts you need to complete an accurate bibliography and to recheck sources if needed.

I have completed research using these sources of information:

_____
_____
_____
_____
_____
_____

☐ **6. Organize research**
Choose three to five main ideas that you would like to communicate with this project.

The main ideas will be:

_____
_____
_____
_____
_____

Choose the information from your research that you feel best supports or illustrates these main ideas. Put an * by the information you will use.

51

☐ **7. Organize Research**
Organize your research information into the main categories by making an outline or categorizing your note cards.

☐ **8. Plan shots**
Decide which pictures or scenes you want to illustrate each idea. Make a list of possible shots.

_____   _____

_____   _____

_____   _____

_____   _____

_____   _____

_____   _____

_____   _____

_____   _____

_____   _____

_____   _____

☐ **9. Make a story board**
Make a story board that shows the general format of each scene. Each frame of the story board should include the narration and a drawing or outline of the shot.

☐ **10. Shoot scenes**
Take the video, slide pictures, or movies. Use these guidelines:
- know how the camera works
- people are usually more interesting to watch than things
- hold the camera still
- keep it simple
- use some unusual angles
- move subjects, not the camera
- if you pan (move the camera), do it slowly and use it mainly to follow a moving subject
- zoom (move in for a close up) slowly
- include close ups of people
- mix action scenes with quieter scenes
- try for different points of view
- shoot a catchy beginning
- shoot a title

☐ **11. Edit**
Edit and organize your shots. Choose those shots that are the best. Delete all unwanted shots. Organize shots to tell your story in the most interesting and informative manner. View your project and make any necessary changes that would improve the quality of your program.

☐ **12. Add audio**
The sound track should include narration, music, words of the announcer or other people, or natural sounds. Write your script to correspond with the visual portion of your project. Try out the audio with the pictures. Make any necessary changes. Add music or sounds that will make your final product more appealing to the audience. Record your final version of the audio.

☐ **13. Show the finished product**

☐ **14. Evaluate**
Use the evaluation form provided by your teacher to evaluate your work on this project.

☐ **15. Application**
    1. What would you add to your multi-media show that would make it more realistic?
    2. If a producer asked you to make a proposal to expand your presentation to make a one-half hour television program, what would you suggest? Write a brief proposal that includes the scope of the program, the intended audience, benefits or appeal to the audience, and possible advertisers.

Story Board

Name _____

Project title _____

1. _____   2. _____   3. _____
_____   _____   _____

4. _____   5. _____   6. _____
_____   _____   _____

7. _____   8. _____   9. _____
_____   _____   _____

Poster Project

Posters are usually large pieces of paper with some combination of pictures and words. Posters are used for many purposes—to advertise products, candidates, movies and happenings, to relay information about common concerns or hazards, to give recognition, or to inform or teach. The common element is that posters should communicate an idea in a bold, attention-getting format.

For this project, you will be creating your own poster that will communicate an idea to other people. Before you begin this project, spend some time looking at posters to get ideas that will help make your poster better. This assignment sheet shows you everything you have to do to produce an attractive, informative poster. Check off each step as you complete it.

☐ **1. Select subject area or topic**

_____

☐ **2. Research** (if assigned)
Use _____ different references to gather information on your topic. Take notes from your research. Keep records of your sources of information, so you will have all of the facts you need to complete an accurate bibliography and to recheck sources if needed. Consider using some of these different sources of information:

- magazine articles, pamphlets, newspapers, and reports
- reference books
- field trip
- books
- movies, slides, filmstrips, videos, or television specials
- charts, tables, graphs, diagrams, collections, or maps
- interview an authority
- experiment or survey
- guided observations
- conferences, seminars, or performances

I have completed research using these sources of information:

_____

_____

_____

_____

3. Focus on main ideas
What is the main idea (or ideas) that you want to communicate with the poster?

_____

4. Decide on Purpose
What is the purpose of your poster? What do you want people to do as a result of seeing this poster? Are you trying to persuade or convince people to do something, to inform, to advertise, to teach, or to start people thinking about something?

The purpose of my poster will be to _____

_____

As a result of seeing my poster people will _____

_____

5. Brainstorm headline
Write several words or phrases you could use as a headline on your poster. Play around with words and phrases until you have a long list of possibilities. Remember that a headline should summarize the idea you are trying to communicate and grab the reader's attention.

_____

_____

_____

_____

_____

_____

6. Select the best headline

7. Plan poster
Plan the way your poster will look by sketching several different possibilities. Think about what kind of picture or illustration will best communicate your idea. Think of different ways to make your poster unique, attractive, and attention-getting.

Consider using special lettering, adding texture, a third dimension or a real object, cutting out a section, making the poster an unusual shape, taking a different perspective, combining elements, or reversing or rearranging elements and positions. Sketch several designs.

☐ **8. Choose the best design**

☐ **9. Make a list of materials**
List all of the materials you will
need. Check off each item as you
get it.

_____

_____

_____

_____

_____

_____

_____

☐ **10. Make poster**
Carefully sketch out your best design on large paper with a light pencil.
Measure so the lines are parallel and level and lettering is even. After you
have finished "roughing in" your design, complete it by adding color.
When you are finished, your poster should be colorful and easy to read
from a distance.

☐ **11. Present your poster**

☐ **12. Evaluation**
Use the evaluation form provided by your teacher to evaluate your work
on this project.

☐ **13. Application**
How else could you present this information? Suggest at least two other
ways. Which way do you think would be most effective?

Problem Solution Project

Problems, problems, problems! There are big problems, little problems, personal problems, problems that concern a lot of people, problems with obvious solutions, and problems that seem to have no solution. The world abounds with problems, all needing creative solutions.

In this project you will get a chance to apply your skills as a problem solver. You will be choosing a problem and carefully working through a solution. This assignment sheet shows you everything you need to think about as you seek the best solution to your chosen problem. Check off each step as you complete it.

☐ **1. Choose a problem**
Choose a problem that you think needs a solution. Look around you and make a list of problems that exist in your personal life, your family, your classroom or school, your community, the state or country you live in, or in the world.

Problem possibilities:

_____

_____

_____

_____

_____

_____

Select one of these problems. State clearly what you think the problem is.

_____

_____

☐ **2. List facts**
Write down everything you know about this problem. Write all the facts that relate to this problem. Find the answers to questions about *who, what, where, when, why, how, how many, and how often.*

58

☐ **3. Research**

After you have listed everything you know about the problem, you may have to collect more information from other sources. Use several different sources to gather more information about your problem. Write down all of your new information and keep records of your sources of information.

I have completed research using these sources of information:

_____
_____
_____
_____
_____
_____
_____
_____
_____

☐ **4. Select important information**

When you have finished your list of information, indicate which information you feel is most significant by putting an * by it.

☐ **5. Restate the problem**

Often after you get more information, you find that the problem is not what you originally thought it was. You will now be trying to state the problem in many different ways. Read carefully through all of the information you collected. Based on all of these facts, how can you restate the problem a different way? What is the real problem? What is the real objective? What must be accomplished? Look at the problem in several different ways. Write the problem several different ways by completing these sentences:

In what way might I/we _____

In what way might I/we _____

In what way might I/we _____

In what way might I/we _____

In what way might I/we _____

In what way might I/we _____

Select the best problem statement from the list above.

The real problem is _____

_____

☐ 6. Brainstorm ideas

Here is your chance to be creative. Write down all the ideas you have for solving this problem. Even if an idea seems silly or impractical, add it to your list, because it might start you thinking about other solutions. Use your imagination and write as many solutions as possible without judging whether the ideas are good or not. Record your ideas on the "Brainstorming" sheet.

☐ 7. Decide on criteria

What are some things involved in determining whether a solution to this problem is good or not? What standards will you use to judge the best solution? Make a list of three to five essential elements of the best solution or considerations or tests that the final solution must pass.

The final solution must meet these criteria:

1. _____

2. _____

3. _____

4. _____

5. _____

☐ 8. Rate solutions

Now you will use your criteria to evaluate your possible solutions.

Fill in the "Solution Grid" by listing your ideas and your criteria. Decide how each idea measures up to each criterion and assign a number to represent that rating. Add the ratings for each idea and record the total in the total column.

☐ 9. Solution finding

Examine all of your ideas. Which ideas have the highest rating? Which ones have the lowest rating? Can some ideas with the lowest ratings be used if they are changed in some way? Can some solutions be combined to make better solutions? Based on this evaluation, which idea looks like it is the most promising solution?

The best solution would be _____

_____

60

☐ **10. Plan of action**
Now you will need to develop a plan of action to help you implement the solution you selected. Use the "Plan of Action" sheet to plan what you will do to complete the solution for your problem.

☐ **11. Take action**
Carry out your plan of action.

☐ **12. Presentation**
Describe for your group what problem you selected, how you arrived at a solution, what the solution is, and what you are doing to carry out the solution.

☐ **13. Evaluation**
Use the evaluation form provided by your teacher to evaluate your work on this project.

☐ **14. Application**
How would your parents' solution to this problem be different from or similar to your solution? How can you explain this?

Brainstorming

Name_____

Problem_____

_____

List all of your ideas that are possible solutions to this problem. S-t-r-e-t-c-h your imagination and think of as many ideas as possible. Write down the unusual and fanciful as well as the practical and obvious solutions.

_____
_____
_____
_____
_____
_____
_____
_____
_____
_____
_____
_____
_____
_____
_____
_____
_____
_____
_____
_____

62

Solution Grid

Name_____

Problem_____

_____

List your possible solutions under "Ideas." Across the top, list the criteria you have selected. Rate each idea or possible solution according to the following scale:

    3 = very good job of meeting criterion
    2 = fair job of meeting criterion
    1 = poor job of meeting criterion
    0 = does not meet criterion at all

If some criteria are more important than others, you may want to "weight" them (or increase their importance) by multiplying all ratings in those columns by a factor of two or three.

Once you have rated all ideas, add up the ratings for each idea and record the total in the column marked "Total." Look at the scores to see which ideas scored the highest. These are your best solutions.

Ideas	Criteria						Total
1. _____							
2. _____							
3. _____							
4. _____							
5. _____							
6. _____							
7. _____							
8. _____							
9. _____							
10. _____							
11. _____							
12. _____							
13. _____							
14. _____							
15. _____							

Put an * by the solutions that do the best job of meeting the criteria.

Plan of Action

Name _____

Problem _____

_____

Solution _____

_____

Use this sheet to plan how you will carry out the solution to your problem. Answer questions as they apply to your situation.

1. What needs to be done?
2. Who needs to be sold on this idea?
3. What might be their objections?
4. How can you overcome their objections?
5. What resources do you need to carry out your solution?
6. Where can you get these resources?
7. Who can give you help?
8. How can you best present your solution?
9. Where do you begin?
10. What do you do next?

WHO! WHAT! WHERE! WHAT! How

Plan of Action

What do you need to do? How will you do it? When does it need to be done? Who do you need to contact? Where do you need to go? Answer these questions by making a plan of action that lists everything that you need to do. In addition, make a timetable that specifies when you will complete each task in your plan of action.

What I will do	Start date	Finish date	Completed

Science Project

Science is a broad and intriguing subject. It includes the study of things smaller than atoms and larger than our galaxy. It includes the study of living organisms as well as rocks and minerals. Perhaps the most interesting aspect of science is that there are still so many unknowns. Scientists are still looking for answers to unsolved mysteries. Science is an active subject, where people are experimenting, questioning, testing, probing, and seeking answers.

This project will give you an opportunity to explore a field of science that you find particularly interesting and to share the results of your investigation with other people in a display. This is an ideal opportunity to find out more about a field of science that interests you. This project will require a combination of research and originality. This assignment sheet shows you everything you need to do to make a unique science project. Check off each step as you complete it.

☐ **1. Choose a field of science**
   I would like to do my science project in the area of _____
   _____

☐ **2. Assess present knowledge**

   _____I know a lot about this topic, but I could learn more.
   _____I know some things about this topic.
   _____I don't know very much about this topic.

☐ **3. Pose questions**
   Make a list of several questions that you could ask about this area of science. Questions should be broad enough so they cannot be answered by a single sentence. They should require research and/or experimentation to arrive at an answer. They should be questions for which you would like the answers.

   _____
   _____
   _____
   _____
   _____

65

☐ **4. Choose the best question**
Choose one question that you feel would be best for a science project.
Topic question_____

_____

☐ **5. Research**
Use _____ different references to gather information on this topic. Take notes from your research. Keep records of your sources of information, so you will have all the facts you need to complete an accurate bibliography and to recheck sources if needed. Consider using some of these different sources of information:
- reference books
- people to talk to or write to
- places to visit
- charts, tables, diagrams, collections
- magazines, pamphlets, reports, newspaper articles
- movies, videos, filmstrips, or television specials
- books
- observations, experiments, or surveys

I have completed research using these sources of information:

_____
_____
_____
_____
_____

☐ **6. Decide what you will do**
Decide what you will do to communicate information from your research, to illustrate a scientific principle or to test a hypothesis. You can consider doing an experiment and recording the results, building a model, collecting specimens, taking photographs, making a series of drawings, building a model environment, or some combination of these projects. Write a brief description of what you plan to do.

I will _____

_____

☐ **7. Make a list of materials**
Make a list of all of the materials you will need. Check off each item as you get it.

_____
_____
_____
_____
_____

66

☐ **8. Get technical assistance**

If you will need any help in carrying out your plans, ask someone with knowledge in this area to help you. Discuss your plans and what kind of help you need.

☐ **9. Make project**

Do whatever you have planned to do for your project. Conduct the experiment, make the model, collect specimens, etc.

If you are conducting an experiment, remember that you must:

- test only one variable at a time
- measure carefully and record your results
- write out your procedure (what you did)
- record the results (what happened) in a chart, table or graph
- draw a conclusion based on the results of your experiment

☐ **10. Write report**

Write a report to accompany your project. This report should include information you found in your research as well as any interesting results from your experiment. It should give people all the information they need to understand your project. Your report should be neatly written and include a title page, bibliography, and table of contents (if assigned).

☐ **11. Make graphic aids**

Make any charts, graphs, or diagrams that will illustrate your project. Make sure they are neat, colorful, easily read, and clearly labeled.

67

☐ **12. Make display**

Make a display of your project that includes the following things:

☐ title (your study question or topic)
☐ your name
☐ report
☐ explanation of your experiment, model, or collection
☐ display - model, collection, experiment set up, samples or specimens, or demonstration apparatus
☐ charts, diagrams, pictures, or model
☐ conclusion - what you learned or what scientific principle was shown
☐ application - explanation of how this information can be used

☐ **13. Present project**

☐ **14. Evaluation**

Use the evaluation form provided by your teacher to evaluate your work on this project.

☐ **15. Application**

1. Explain how this information can be used. When would you ever have to know this? To what does it relate?

2. What are some things that we don't know about this area of science?

Special Event Project

Special events can be parties, celebrations, historical reminders, commemorations, special-theme days, reenactments, or fund raisers. They are opportunities for people to get together for a special reason.

For this exiting project you will be planning some sort of special event. It could be a fair, parade, festival, or special day. Because special events involve many people, they require more organization than most projects. The end result, however, is a celebration that many people can enjoy.

This assignment sheet shows you everything you have to do to plan and carry out a special event. Check off each step as you complete it.

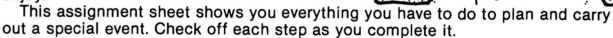

☐ **1. Select theme**
Decide what your special event will celebrate or demonstrate.

Theme - _____

☐ **2. Assess present knowledge**

_____ I know a lot about this topic, but I could learn more.
_____ I know some things about this topic.
_____ I don't know very much about this topic.

☐ **3. Research**
Use _____ different references to gather information on your topic. Take notes from your research. Keep records of your sources of information. Consider using some of these different sources of information:

- magazine articles, pamphlets, newspapers, and reports
- reference books (encyclopedias, etc.)
- field trip
- books
- movies, slides, filmstrips, videos, or television specials
- interview an authority on the subject
- conferences, seminars, or performances

I have completed research using these sources of information:

_____

_____

_____

_____

69

☐ **4. Brainstorm**
   Brainstorm a list of things you could do.
   Consider things like food, games, dances,
   singing, plays or skits, athletic events,
   intellectual contests, poetry readings,
   demonstrations, fashion shows, arts and
   crafts displays, monologues, character
   portrayals, and things that people can do.

BRAINSTORM LIST
1. GAMES
2. FOOD & DRINK
3. SINGING
4. Pl

   Possible activities:

   _____
   _____
   _____
   _____
   _____
   _____
   _____
   _____
   _____
   _____
   _____

   Continue on another piece of paper if you need more room.

☐ **5. Select the best ideas**
   Put an * by your best ideas. Select those activities that will best carry
   out your theme and also provide an interesting learning experience for
   participants.

☐ **6. Decide on presentation**
   Decide on the best way to present these ideas. Consider ideas like a
   reenactment, festival, parade, fair, simulation, feast, or special
   presentation.

   My presentation will be_____
   _____

☐ **7. Draft a plan for your special event**
   List tentative times, dates, activities,
   participants, places, and anything else that
   describes your event. Include the cost of the
   event and how it will be funded.

DRAFT
Special Event
1.
2.
3.
4.
DATE:
TIME:
NOTE

☐ **8. Get permission**
   Present your plan to the proper authorities
   for approval. Make any necessary revisions.
   Take the revised plan back for approval if
   necessary.

70

□ **9. Arrange for facilities**

Reserve any facilities you will need—classrooms, gymnasium, field, patio, or stage. Also think about whether you will need special seating or different arrangements of areas. Make arrangements for these special set-ups.

□ **10. Divide and conquer**

Divide the event into individual activities. Describe in detail what is to be done, who is to do it, and when it is to be done.

□ **11. Contact resources**

Make a list of all of the people who will help with the organization and preparations, or who will make presentations or serve as resources for your special event. Contact each person and ask for their help. Keep careful records of who will do what. Check back with the people periodically.

_____

_____

_____

_____

_____

_____

_____

□ **12. Make a list of materials**

Make a list of all of the materials, ingredients, and supplies you will need. Check off each item as you get it.

_____

_____

_____

_____

_____

_____

_____

_____

_____

□ **13. Send out invitations or announcements**

□ 14. Make preparations

Make all necessary preparations. Write scripts, organize people, make posters, sew costumes, construct props, banners, or scenery, cook food, arrange publicity, or make games. Make a list of everything that needs to be done. Assign people to each task. Communicate deadlines and any special instructions to the people who will complete each task.

□ 15. Check back with resource people

Contact each person who will play an important part in your special event. Make sure they know their part and will be available and ready when they are needed.

□ 16. Make presentation

□ 17. Evaluate

Use the evaluation form provided by your teacher to evaluate your work on this project.

□ 18. Application

1. If some aliens from a different planet came to your event, what would they think? Write a one-paragraph report that they might send back to their planet that gives their impression of the activities.
2. Compose an original song to sing at your special event.

Special Event Planning Sheet

Event _____

What needs to be done	Who will do it	Finish by (date)	Completed

Speech/Oral Report Project

No matter who you are and what you do, you will have many opportunities throughout your life to speak in front of a group of people. Whether you are making an announcement to a small group of classmates or addressing a large assembly of strangers, you will need to present your ideas in a manner that is organized, interesting, and memorable. Giving a speech is just one way to communicate information to other people, but because it's a live presentation, it can be made more interesting than presenting the same information in a written report. In order to get your ideas across to your audience, you must clearly define your topic, select information, and arrange your facts in an organized manner.

In this project you will be selecting a topic and then giving a speech or oral report to your class on this topic. This assignment sheet shows you everything you have to do to prepare and deliver and successful speech. Check off each step as you complete it.

☐ **1. Choose a topic**
   Select a topic that you are interested in and that your audience will find interesting. It should be a topic that is not too broad, or you will need to talk a long time just to give the audience an overview of the topic. It also should not be so specific or narrow that you will not be able to find enough information to make an interesting speech. You should be able to state the main theme of your speech in one short, clear, concise sentence.

   My speech will be _____

   _____

☐ **2. Decide on the purpose of your speech**
   Decide what you want to accomplish with your speech. Do you want to convince or persuade, inform or teach, entertain, describe, arouse an emotion, or inspire people to do something?

   The purpose of my speech will be to _____

   _____

☐ 3. Assess present knowledge

_____I know a lot about his topic, but I could learn more.
_____I know some things about this subject.
_____I don't know very much about this topic.

☐ 4. Research

Use _____ different references to gather information on your topic. Take notes from your research. Keep records of your sources of information, so you will have all of the facts you need to complete an accurate bibliography and to recheck sources if needed or to quote the source in your speech. Consider using some of these different sources of information:

- magazine articles, pamphlets, newspapers, and reports
- reference books (encyclopedias, etc.)
- field trip
- books
- movies, slides, filmstrips, videos, or television specials
- charts, tables, graphs, diagrams, collections, or maps
- interview an authority
- experiment or survey
- guided observations
- conferences, seminars, or performances
- other _____

I have completed research using these sources of information:

_____

_____

_____

_____

☐ 5. Decide on format

Decide on the most appropriate format for your speech. You may choose to simply stand in front of your audience and speak. You may want to use visual aids. You may demonstrate something, or you may want to have the audience take part in an activity.

My speech will_____

☐ 6. Make an outline

Plan your speech by writing a brief outline. Limit your speech to three to five main points. Your basic plan for your speech should include an attention-getting beginning, a stimulating middle, and an effective end. Use subheadings for details, supporting information, or examples that support the major points.

☐ **7. Write your speech**
Refer to the guidelines for writing a speech. Then write out what you will want to say in your speech using these guidelines.

☐ **8. Prepare speech notes**
Copy your speech on notecards or prepare a detailed outline of your speech. You will use these speech notes to remind you what to say during your speech, so they should be written in large letters. If you use note cards, number each card to indicate the correct order. If you will use visual aids, make a note on your outline or cards of when to present them.

☐ **9. Prepare visual aids**
Visual aids should be used to show how things look, how they work, or how they relate to each other. Visual aids should only be used to illustrate information in your speech and should not detract from what you are saying. Any visual aids should be attractive and easy to see.

Make any necessary preparations of visual aids, charts, props, or examples.

☐ **10. Edit**
Cut out any unnecessary repetitions. Check vocabulary to make sure you have used descriptive words and phrases. Check grammar and usage. Make any necessary corrections that will improve your speech.

☐ **11. Practice**
Refer to the guidelines for delivering a speech. Keep these guidelines in mind as you rehearse your speech. Read your speech out loud and time it. Use a tape recorder to record it. Stand in front of a mirror to practice. Ask a friend or one of your parents to listen to your speech and give you helpful criticism. Revise your speech, if necessary, and practice it again.

☐ **12. Present speech**

☐ **13. Evaluate**
Use the evaluation form provided by your teacher to evaluate your work on this project.

☐ **14. Application**
What are some controversial issues associated with this topic? How do you feel about these issues? Where could you get more information?

Guidelines for Writing a Speech

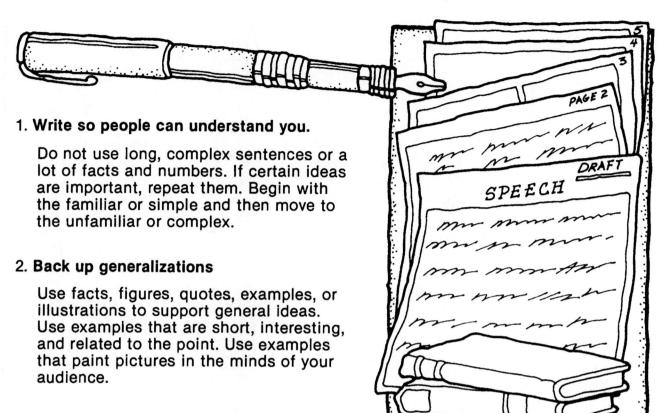

1. **Write so people can understand you.**

   Do not use long, complex sentences or a lot of facts and numbers. If certain ideas are important, repeat them. Begin with the familiar or simple and then move to the unfamiliar or complex.

2. **Back up generalizations**

   Use facts, figures, quotes, examples, or illustrations to support general ideas. Use examples that are short, interesting, and related to the point. Use examples that paint pictures in the minds of your audience.

3. **Write for feeling**

   Write something you can express with feeling. You don't want to sound like you are reading out of a book. Use descriptive words. Replace trite, over-used phrases with vivid, unique phrases.

4. **Be organized**

   Each point should relate to the main theme of the speech or to a preceding point.

5. **The introduction should be an attention-grabber**

   Capture the interest of your audience with an opening that helps them visualize what you will be talking about and also stirs their interest in hearing more about the topic.

6. **Plan a strong ending**

   Give the audience something to think about, a brief summary, a look to the future, a possible solution, your feelings, or a call to action. Make it strong and memorable.

Guidelines for Delivering a Speech

1. **Body language is important**

   Stand tall and do away with any habits or accessories that will be distracting. Do not fidget or play with clothing or jewelry. Appear confident.

2. **Establish eye contact**

   Look at people in all sections of the audience.

3. **Use a strong, pleasant voice**

   Talk like you usually do but with a strong, loud voice so people can hear you.

4. **No inappropriate joking or laughing**

   Do not detract from your main theme with jokes or comments that draw the audience's attention to other things.

5. **Add variety**

   Vary you pace (how fast you speak), pitch (how high or low), and volume (loud or soft).

6. **Know what you will say**

   Rehearse your speech and have notes on what to say. Choose words that will be interesting and easily understood.

7. **Be organized**

   Try to anticipate anything you will need and have it ready.

8. **Anticipate questions**

   Think about what questions your audience might ask and have answers ready.

Survey Project

Surveys are commonly used to find out how people feel about certain things or how they behave. By asking a small, select group of people (a sample), surveyors try to draw conclusions about a much larger group. If you are careful about how you word the questions and how you select the people to be interviewed in the survey, you can sometimes generalize the results of the survey to a larger segment of the population.

In this project you will be conducting a survey on the topic of your choice. This assignment sheet shows you everything you must do to construct an accurate survey. Check off each step as you complete it.

☐ **1. Review the guidelines for conducting a survey**
Before you begin work on your survey, you will need some basic information about conducting a survey. Read through the guidelines for conducting a survey.

☐ **2. Choose a general topic**
What are you trying to find out? Select a general question or topic of interest._____

_____

☐ **3. Choose sample**
Describe the large or general population that you are trying to get information about.

_____

_____

Decide how you can get a representative sample of this group. Describe the sample you will survey that is representative of this general population.

My sample population will be _____

_____

_____

I will survey approximately _____ people.

☐ **4. Choose subtopics**
Break your general topic into smaller parts by choosing two to four subtopics. These should be questions or issues that relate directly to your general topic.

_____

_____

_____

_____

☐ **5. Write questions**
Write several questions for each subtopic. Write more questions than you think you will use. Try wording the same question several different ways. Write your questions on a separate piece of paper.

☐ **6. Select questions**
When you have a long list of questions, select the best ones. Try to present an equal number of questions for each topic.

☐ **7. Make questionnaire**
Write the questions on a questionnaire. Mix up the questions so that all the questions on one topic are not grouped together.

☐ **8. Take survey**
Either hand out copies of your questionnaire and have people complete it and return it to you or use the questionnaire to interview each person in your sample. You will need to keep careful records of all answers and make sure all questionnaires are returned to you.

☐ **9. Tabulate answers**
Collect all of your data and organize it, so you will know how many people gave each response. Categorize answers according to each subtopic.

☐ **10. Make graphic representation**
Put your information into some kind of chart or graph that will visually show the results of your survey.

☐ **11. Draw conclusions**

Analyze the results of your survey. What does the data tell you about your sample of people? Can you generalize to a larger population? Do you think the results are valid?

Based on the results of this survey_____

_____

_____

_____

_____

☐ **12. Written presentation of findings**

Write a brief one to two-page summary of your survey. Include in the summary the following items:

- the general question
- copy of questionnaire
- description of general population
- description of sample
- tabulation of data
- graphic representation of data
- conclusions

☐ **13. Present project**

☐ **14. Evaluation**

Use the evaluation form provided by your instructor to evaluate your work on this project.

☐ **15. Application**

Of what value is this information? How could it be used? Who would be interested in knowing this?

Survey Guidelines

1. **Questions cannot be biased.**
   The way you word a question must not lead the person answering it to favor one answer over another. Write questions so that all answers are equal possibilities.

2. **Provide an answer for those people who do not have an answer.**
   Include a response like "Don't care," "No Opinion," or "Does not apply."

3. **Ask the same question several different ways.**
   Find different ways to ask for the same information. This way if your questions are biased, they will be balanced out by other questions that ask the same thing but are worded differently.

4. **Limit the number of things you are trying to find out.**
   If you try to survey many different things, you will have a very long questionnaire and your results will be confusing. Choose two or three things that you want to investigate and write several questions for each point.

5. **Your sample must be truly random or truly representative**
   When you are able to interview thousands of people for your survey, you may select them randomly. Usually, however, you will be using a much smaller sample, so you cannot use the random-sample method. Instead, you must select your sample so that it is representative of the larger group. If you want a sample that is representative of the students in your school, you must select people so that the sample represents all grades and the actual percentage of girls and boys or racial backgrounds that you would find in the whole school.

6. **You cannot throw out any responses.**
   You must take all responses into consideration—even ones you don't like or that don't fit in with other results.

7. **You must organize your data.**
   After you have collect responses you need to organize the data so you can make sense out of it. This means tallying the results and putting them in a table, chart, or graph.

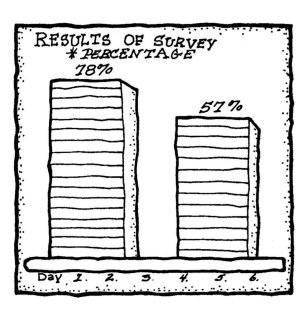

8. **Look at the statistical significance of your results.**
   This means looking at the percentage of people who chose each response and deciding if the percentage is large enough to support saying that one choice is favored more than another.

Written Report Project

Often during your school and work experiences, you will be asked to write a written report or research paper. It is important to be able to communicate ideas to other people in a clear, organized manner. This type of writing is different from writing a story or a poem. Your goal will be to communicate certain facts, concepts, or ideas in a concise, easy-to-read manner.

For this project, you will be selecting a topic and writing a paper on it. You will be required to do more than copy excerpts from various reference materials. You must analyze the information you collect and add some of your own thoughts or opinions. This will make the written product more interesting to the reader, and the project will be more meaningful to you. This assignment sheet shows you everything you need to do for this project. Check off each step as you complete it.

☐ 1. **Select a topic**
    Select a broad topic that you find interesting and that you think you could find adequate information about.

    My topic is _____

☐ 2. **Assess present knowledge**

    _____I know a lot about this topic, but I could learn more.
    _____I know some things about this topic.
    _____I don't know very much about this topic.

☐ 3. **Ask questions**
    Write down several questions about this topic that could be the basis of a research project. These questions should require thoughtful investigation. They should not be questions that can be answered by copying a sentence (or even a paragraph) from a reference book.

    _____

    _____

    _____

    _____

    _____

83

☐ **4. Select research question**
Choose the research question that you think would be most interesting and challenging to answer.

My research question is _____

_____

☐ **5. Research**
Use _____ different references to gather information on your topic. Choose sources that will provide the most up-to-date, complete, and accurate information on your topic. Record notes from your research. Keep records of your sources of information, so you will have all of the facts you need to complete an accurate bibliography and to recheck sources if needed. Consider using some of these different sources of information:

- magazine articles, pamphlets, newspapers, and reports
- reference books
- field trip
- books
- movies, slides, filmstrips, videos, or television specials
- charts, tables, graphs, diagrams, collections, or maps
- interview an authority

- experiment or survey
- guided observations
- conferences, seminars, or performances

I have completed research using these sources of information:

_____

_____

_____

_____

_____

☐ **6. Organize research**
There are several ways to organize information. Some of these ways are chronological (by time), cause-and-effect, and problem-solution. Choose one of these ways to organize information or some other way that is more fitting to the information you have collected and organize your research notes into a few main categories.

Main topics are:

_____

_____

_____

_____

_____

☐ **7. Write rough draft**
Refer to the guidelines for writting a report. Then write the first draft of your report using your main topics as the backbone of the report. Supplement the main topics. with facts, figures, examples, your ideas, different opinions, and background information. Double space so you can easily make changes.

☐ **8. Edit**
Read your report out loud. It should sound natural and smooth. Read your report silently, editing for content, spelling, and grammar. Make any necessary corrections.

☐ **9. Rewrite**
Rewrite or type your report in its final form. Carefully read each page to make sure you have not introduced any new mistakes.

☐ **10. Make visual aids**
Visual aids are helpful in illustrating facts and relationships. Make any charts, graphs, illustrations, or maps that will make your report more interesting and easy to understand.

☐ **11. Add final touches**
Make sure that your report has the following items and that they are in the proper form.
  - ☐ title page
  - ☐ table of contents (only if report is long and divided into several sections)
  - ☐ written report
  - ☐ visual aids
  - ☐ bibliography
  - ☐ cover (includes title, author, any other relevant information, and an attractive picture or design)

☐ **12. Evaluation**
Use the evaluation form provided by your teacher to evaluate your work on this project.

☐ **13. Application**
What are some possibilities for the future for the topic you have selected? State several possibilities and for each one, state a consequence (what other thing might happen if this possibility were to occur).

Guidelines for Writing a Report

1. **Introduction should be attention-getting**
   Your introduction should introduce the reader to the topic and spark interest in finding out more about it.

2. **Write to be understood**
   Express your ideas as clearly as possible. Use simple, easy-to-understand sentences.

3. **Be organized**
   Stick to your main topics. Relate each idea to the main topic or to other ideas. One topic should flow into the next.

4. **Add your own ideas**
   Add your own touch of originality to the report by comparing information, interpreting facts, connecting related ideas, stating a hypothesis, summarizing data, projecting into the future, offering a criticism, suggesting improvements, forming a judgement, defending a position, suggesting a plan or solution, adding new ideas, or weighing the evidence.

5. **Balance fact and emotion**
   Create interest by using a balance of factual information and human-interest perspectives.

6. **Conclusion**
   Tie everything together in a few brief but memorable statements.

How to Write a Works Cited Page

In order to give the reader complete information about your resources, you must include a list of sources you used. This is an important part of a research project. Be sure it is complete, accurate and consistent in form.

Guidelines for works cited

1. Items such as books and articles are arranged in alphabetical order according to the last name of the author(s).

2. If a book has more that one author, the names of the second and third authors are written first name first.

3. Do not number items.

4. If the book or article does not include the author's name, then place the works alphabetically by the first word of their titles, unless the first word is "the," "an," or "a." In these cases, the second word determines the alphabetical order.

5. When a listing takes up more than one line, the second line should be indented.

6. The author's name is followed by a period. The name of the book is followed by a period. A colon separates the place of publication and the name of the publisher. Other information in the entry is separated by commas. A period is placed at the end of the entry.

7. Entries for books do not include page references. Entries for parts of books, magazine articles, or newspaper articles give page numbers.

Book
- name of the author (last name first)
- title of the book (underlined)
- number of volumes, if more than one
- place of publication
- publisher
- date of publication

Periodical
- name of author (last name first)
- title of the article (in quotation marks)
- title of the periodical (underlined)
- volume number or date of publication
- page numbers

Encyclopedia
- title of the article
- name of the encyclopedia
- edition

Interview
- name of the person interviewed
- the words "Personal interview"
- date of the interview

Letter
- name of the author
- the words "Letter to the author"
- date

World Wide Web

Because resources on the World Wide Web vary in content and format, listings will vary slightly depending on the type of site that is used. Resources from the Internet should include as much of the following information as applicable.

- name of author or compiler
- title of the article (in quotation marks)
- title of the book (underlined)
- title of the project or database
- date last updated
- name of the organization sponsoring the site
- date the site was accessed
- the electronic address (URL).

Works Cited Sample Entries

Books, one author

Hopkins, Jane. All About Cats. New York: McMillian, 1995.

Books, two authors

Holmes, Joseph and Thompson, Emily. What Everyone Should Know about Traveling. New York: Poor Man Publications, 2001.

Computer Software

Ho, Helen. Computation Made Easy. Ver. 1.3. Computer software. London: CompuLearning, 2000.

Encyclopedia

"Sitting Bull," World Book Encyclopedia. 2001 ed.

Interview

Bannon, James. Interview. Oak Ridge, TN. 7 May 2002.

Will, Susan. Interview. Fifty Percent. National Public Radio. Washington, D.C. 25, Sept. 1999.

Magazine

Cook, Donna. "Horse Racing in Kentucky." Time 14 January 2002: 56-58.

Letters

Braggett, Jan. Letter to the author. 15 October 2001.

Brochure

James, Katherine. Common Ear Diseases. Department of Health, Education and Welfare. New York: 2002.

Newspaper Article

Pallmetto, Joanna. "Smoking is Hazardous to Your Health." New York Times 22 April 2000: B56.

Television Show

"Our Star – the Sun." Science Today. PBS. WINN, Cincinnati. 31 October 2002.

Face the Nation. Narr. Walter Smith. NBC. WACK, New York. 13 Jan 2002.

World Wide Web

Staton, Julie. "Great White Sharks." Northeast Aquarium Education Project. 2001, 3 March 2001.
< http://www.neaquarium.org/educ/sharks/info>